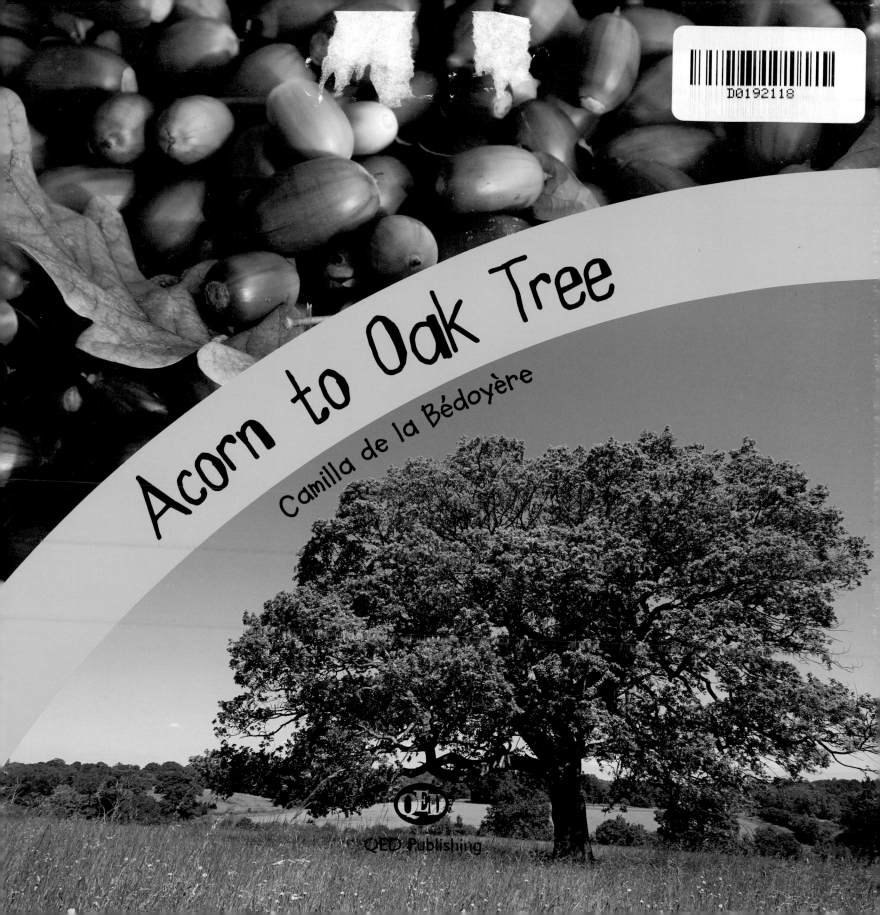

Acorn to Oak Tree

Camilla de la Bédoyère

QED Publishing

Words in **bold** are explained in the Glossary on page 22.

Editor Alexandra Koken
Designer and Picture Researcher Melissa Alaverdy

Picture credits
(t=top, b=bottom, l=left, r=right, c=centre)

Alamy 1b Mike Stone, 9 CuboImages srl, 16 br MichaelGrantsPlants, 17 Natural Visions, 24 William Leaman

Corbis 15b Simko, 18b, 18t, 19t Gerolf Kalt, 21bl Fernando Bengoechea

Getty front cover Karin Smeds/Gorilla Creative Images, 4l Leonard Gertz/Stone, 5t Steve Gorton/Dorling Kindersley, 12bl Steve Gorton/Dorling Kindersley

Hawk Conservancy Trust 14

Nature Picture Library 20bl Stephen Dalton

Photolibrary 4-5 Naturfoto Online, 11tl Richard Packwood, 11 James Osmond, 12br Breck P Kent, 17tr Brendt Fischer, 19 Justus de Cuveland, 20 FB-Rose, 21 Nick Cable

Science Photo Library 15t Bruno Petriglia, 16l Dr Jeremy Burgess

Shutterstock back cover kosam, 1t mcseem, 2tl Le Do, 3t SunnyCatty, 5b aleks.k, 8-9 alexnika, 10bl kaczor58, 10 b kaczor58, 10t Fotofermer, 12tr Florin C, 13t Diana Tallun, 13 Pling, 22 Yuliyan Velchev, 23 slowfish, 24 Le Do

Contents

What is an oak tree?

An oak is a type of tree.
All trees are plants, and they
have roots, stems and leaves.

Trees are plants that grow
tall and strong. Their
woody stems are
called **trunks**.
A thick layer of
bark protects
the trunk.

leaves

stem

roots

⇧ The oak's roots take water from the ground.

Oak trees grow all
over the world. They
can grow very tall.

branches

trunk

⇨ Trees have woody trunks
that are covered with bark.

bark

⇦ Branches
are covered with leaves.

5

The story of an oak tree

Oak trees grow in forests, woods, gardens and parks. They live for a long time.

When they are between 40 and 50 years old, oaks start to grow seeds, called **acorns**. One day, new oaks will grow from the acorns.

2

seedling

⇧ A new plant grows. It is called a seedling.

1

acorn

⇦ An acorn is a seed.

3

sapling

The story of how a small acorn can grow into a huge tree is called a **life cycle**.

4

tree

⇧ As the plant grows taller it is called a sapling.

⇨ Small acorns grow into big oak trees.

Little acorns

New acorns have a green skin. As they get older, their skin becomes dry and brown.

cupule

Each acorn is a seed from which a new oak tree will grow one day. Some acorns have a little stalk. Others grow on twigs.

Acorns have stiff little cups called **cupules**. When they are ripe, acorns fall from the tree.

⇦ Cupules of an English oak hang from stalks.

⇧ Turkey oaks have cupules with spikes.

The first shoot

Acorns need air, water and warmth to grow.

Once an acorn falls on the ground, the skin cracks open and a tiny root appears. This is called **germination**.

Some acorns germinate in **autumn**. Others germinate in the spring, or even a few years later.

⇧ Small leaves grow on the seedling.

⇦ Next, a green shoot appears.

⇦ Roots grow down into the soil.

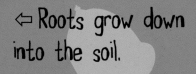

The shoot grows towards the sun. Once little leaves appear, this small plant is called a **seedling**.

5

⇧ As the seedling grows, more leaves appear.

⇨ The leaves open out in the sunshine.

11

Growing tall

Seedlings grow taller.
Soon they become **saplings**.

Saplings have many leaves. They
need sunlight, air and water to
grow even bigger.

⇨ Saplings grow
faster when
there is lots
of sunshine.

2

⇧ Oak trees grow about
50 centimetres taller every year.

1

⇨ You can tell how old
a tree is by counting
the rings in its trunk.

12

⇧ As the tree gets older, it grows more branches.

The tree trunk gets thicker and taller every year.

4

⇨ Oaks grow slowly, but they grow big and strong.

Catkins

Oak trees have two types of flowers. They have female flowers and male flowers.

Male flowers are called **catkins**. They are covered in little yellow grains called pollen.

Female oak flowers are much smaller. They hold the tree's **eggs**.

⇧ Female oak flowers are tiny and hard to see.

14

Pollen grains are very small. They are like grains of yellow dust.

catkins

⇨ Catkins are long and hang from the branch in clumps.

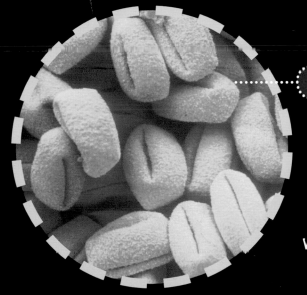

pollen grain

⇦ Catkins are covered with pollen grains.

A new acorn grows

The wind blows pollen off the catkins. Some of the pollen is blown onto female flowers.

Tiny grains of pollen land on the female flowers. One grain of pollen joins with each egg. This is called **fertilization**.

When the eggs are fertilized they can grow into new seeds, or acorns.

pollen grains

⇧ Pollen grains are so small and light the wind can carry them.

1

⇨ Thousands of acorns can grow on one tree.

Acorns ripen in the autumn.
Many forest animals eat them.

⇨ Hungry squirrels eat
acorns in the autumn.

⇩ The ripe acorns change
colour, from green to brown.

2

Time to rest

In winter, the trees and the acorns are resting. They wait for warm weather.

In spring, there is sunlight and warmth. The acorns grow into seedlings, and new leaves grow on the trees.

In summer, new acorns grow and the life cycle begins again.

2

spring

1

winter

3

summer

In autumn, most trees and plants are getting ready to rest. The leaves on the oak trees change colour and die.

4

The ripe acorns and leaves fall to the forest ground.

⇐ Old leaves turn red or brown.

autumn

Growing old

Old oak trees are full of living things. They are home to many animals and plants.

An oak tree can live for hundreds of years. Even when it dies, it is still a home for many living things.

⇨ Insects live in oak trees. Wasps chew the wood and use it to make their nests.

wasp nest ....

20

⇧ Squirrels and birds, such as this barn owl, build nests in old tree trunks.

Some old oaks are cut down for their wood, or **timber**. Wood is used to make floorboards, doors, pencils and even paper.

⇦ An oak tree can live for hundreds of years.

⇨ Oak timber is used to make furniture, such as tables and chairs.

21

Glossary

Acorn
An oak seed.

Autumn
The season between summer and winter.

Bark
The hard layer on the outside of a tree trunk.

Catkins
Male flowers on a tree.

Cupule
The little cup on an acorn.

Egg
The female part of a plant.

Fertilization
When a grain of pollen joins with an egg.

Germination
When a seed begins to grow.

Life cycle
The story of how a living thing changes from birth to death, and how it has young, or makes seeds that grow into new plants.

Pollen
Yellow dust that is made by male flowers, or catkins.

Sapling
A young tree with leaves.

Seedling
A young plant that has grown from a seed.

Timber
The wood from a tree that is used to make things.

Trunk
The woody stem of a tree.

Index

Notes for parents and teachers

- Look through the book and talk about the pictures. Read the captions and ask questions about the things in the photographs that have not been mentioned in the text.

- Help your child to find out more about plants and their life cycles with hands-on science. It is easy to grow most beans and many flower seeds, and watch their life cycles unfold in just one or two seasons.

- It is possible to germinate acorns and grow oak trees from them. The best way to do this is to research what types of oak grow well in your area, and what conditions those particular acorns need to germinate. Attempt to grow several trees, as not all will germinate or survive to the sapling stage.

- Visit woodlands together and talk about the habitat. Draw pictures or take photographs of animals and plants that live in a woodland habitat. Look out for the stages of plant life cycles, such as seeds, fruits, seedlings and flowers.

- Make a family tree together and use it to talk about time and relationships. Children find it hard to imagine that adults were once young. Show them photographs, and share your memories of childhood, to help them to understand time, and how people change.

24